CHALLENGING
BRAIN
TWISTERS

D1531196

CHALLENGING

BRAIN TWISTERS

— 100 —
LOGIC AND NUMBER PUZZLES

FRED COUGHLIN

Skyhorse Publishing

Skyhorse Publishing books may be purchased in bulk at special discounts for sales promotion, corporate gifts, fund-raising, or educational purposes. Special editions can also be created to specifications. For details, contact the Special Sales Department, Skyhorse Publishing, 307 West 36th Street, 11th Floor, New York, NY 10018 or info@skyhorsepublishing.com.

Skyhorse® and Skyhorse Publishing® are registered trademarks of Skyhorse Publishing, Inc.®, a Delaware corporation.

Visit our website at www.skyhorsepublishing.com.

10 9 8 7 6 5 4 3 2

Library of Congress Cataloging-in-Publication Data is available on file.

Cover design by Brian Peterson

ISBN: 978-1-5107-4681-7

Printed in the United States of America

Contents

Introduction

Since I was a little kid, puzzles have always been an integral part of my life. Some of my earliest memories include sitting at my grandmother's kitchen table and trying to solve the remaining puzzles from her magazines, or solving the weekly word search from the Sunday paper with my parents or uncles. As I grew older, the love of puzzles continued to grow, and I explored not just solving but also crafting puzzles, publishing some word searches in my high school newspaper.

As an adult, my appreciation for puzzles has blossomed further. I've used the concepts in solving these puzzles in other areas in my life, whether it was developing algorithms in computer science, or even devising alternate ways to approach problems in chemistry. Puzzles have even become an important part of our family, as I watch the unique ways that my three daughters approach solving puzzles. The most interesting part of this is that it's not a one-way street; I may plan to teach them a potential solving path, but then they surprise me and show me a completely different idea I hadn't considered!

Puzzle solving has become a regular part of my life, encompassing many aspects that I would never have imagined years ago. Practicing puzzles has helped me exercise my brain and taught me to think outside the box to find other solution paths. I hope these puzzles will help you to exercise your brain as well, and to think outside the box in your life.

—Fred Coughlin

How to Solve the Puzzles

Catwalk Example

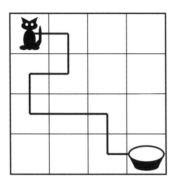

In the Catwalk puzzles featured in this book, we need to find a path from the cat to its milk bowl; each step in the path will move either horizontally or vertically, and will never revisit a previously visited cell. Clues outside the grid indicate the number of cells that the cat's path visits in the row or column. In some puzzles, these clues may be omitted. Some puzzles also have multiple cats and bowls; determining which bowl belongs to which cat is a part of the puzzle.

Looking at the top row with the clue of 2, only two of the cells can be used in the path, one of which is the cell the cat starts in. If the cat moves straight down at the start, it will have to return to the top row later but will get stranded; it won't be able to move left or right, and it can't double back on its path. Thus, the only way it can start is to move to the right, and then down out of that row.

At this point, we can work backwards from the bowl. The rightmost column has a clue of 1, so we know the only cell visited in it is the cat's bowl. Therefore, we must move left. The next column has a clue of 2, so we know we must move up one from there.

We are now in the third column from the left, third row down. The clue we have for that row is 3 and we cannot repeat cells, so we must move left two more cells. From there, our only choice is up 1, into the second row. That row has a clue of 2, meaning we must move to the right. We can now move up 1 to rejoin and complete the path.

Easy as ABC Example

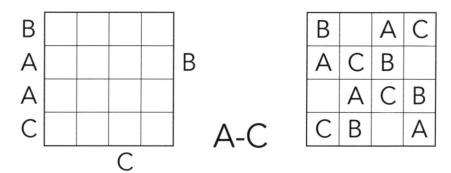

For the ABC puzzles featured in this book, we need to place letters into the grid such that each row contains the indicated letters, which in this example are A–C, as noted on the lower right. Each letter can only be used once in each row or column. As the grid is 4x4, this means there will also be one empty space in each row and column. Letters outside the grid indicate the first letter seen from that direction.

Looking at the left side of the grid, we see that there is only one row that starts with a B and one row that starts with a C. Since each letter must appear once in every column, the only place that we can put the B in the leftmost column is in the top row. Similarly, the only place we can put the C in that column is the bottom row.

Having filled the C in the bottom row, we can look at column 3. The first letter in that row is a C, but there can't be a C in the bottom row there because we've already placed the C in column 1. This means that the bottom cell in column C is a blank, and we can place the C in the third row. As we placed the B in row 1 already, we can fill in the rest of column 3.

Looking at row 2, we know that because B is in the third column, the blank is in the fourth column. As the row starts with A, we can complete that row. Doing so places the blank for column 1 in row 3, allowing us to fill in that row and place the rest of the letters into the puzzle.

Fill-In Example

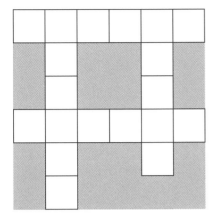

Astros

Braves

Expos

Red Sox

In the Fill-In puzzles featured in this book, we are given words to fit into grids, similar to traditional crossword puzzles. In this example, we have to fit four baseball teams into the grid. One possible approach is to start by looking at the top row. With six cells, we can see that three of the four teams can fit into the top row. The second letter of that row must be the start of a different six-letter word. The only word that fits in this case is BRAVES. With that added, we can now fill in the two words going down (REDSOX and EXPOS), and the final word going across.

Grades Example

	2	1	1	1	1	
1						9
1						4
2						12
0						0
2						8
	18	5	4	3	3	

9				
		4		
9				3
	5		3	

In a Grades puzzle, we have to write some single-digit numbers into the grid. A box with a number cannot touch another box with a number either horizontally, vertically, or diagonally. That means cells will be left blank. Above and to the left of the grid, the given clues tell us how many numbers are in each column or row. The bottom and right clues correspond to the sum of the numbers in that column or row.

We see that the fourth row from the top has a clue of zero, so we know no numbers will be in that row. From the clues for column 1, we see that it has 2 digits that equal 18 when added together. The only way to do that is for both of those digits to be 9. Where can we place them? The sum of the digits in rows 2, 4, and 5 are all less than 9, so they cannot go there. Therefore, we can place the digit 9 into rows 1 and 3 of column 1.

The clues tell us that column 2 has 1 digit that equals 5, so it is 5. Digits in the puzzle cannot touch each other horizontally, vertically, or diagonally. This means that no digit can be in the top four cells of column 2, as they would be touching the two 9s that we placed. This means we must place 5 into the bottom cell of column 2.

The number in row 2 has 1 digit that equals 4, so it must be a 4. It can't be in columns 4 or 5 as they both add up to 3. Thus, we must place the 4 in column 3. The two digits in row 3 must add up to 12; as we wrote a 9 in column 1 already, the other digit must be 3. As digits cannot touch, the only spot we can place this is in column 5. Finally, we place the second digit of row 5, which must be 3, according to our clues—there is one digit, and it adds up to 3—in column 4.

Kakuro Example

Kakuro puzzles have been popular in the Japanese puzzling community for many years, even before the recent rise in popularity of sudoku. The kakuro puzzle is essentially a numerical crossword, in which clues above and to the left of the grid indicate the sum of the digits in each number. The number above a diagonal line tells the sum of the digits in the cells immediately to its right. The number below the diagonal tells the sum of the cells immediately below it. Digits cannot repeat within a sum, and only single digits may be used.

To begin with, let us look at the second row. The 30 indicates the sum of the digits that will go in that row. For a sum of 30, there is only one way to write it with four unique single digits: 9+8+7+6. Similarly, for 10 in the third row, the only way to write that with four unique single digits is 1+2+3+4. Thus, these will be the digits in those rows, in some order. To determine that order, the clue in column 1 is 13. The only way to use a digit from the 30 and the 10 is to use 9 and 4, so we place those in rows 2 and 3 respectively. Using the remaining digits, only 8 plus 3 equals 11 in column 4, so we place the 11 there.

Let us now examine column 2. The four digits must add up to 26. We know that row 2 must be a 7 or 6, and row 3 must be a 1 or 2. We can't choose a 1, because 1+9+8+7 equals only 24. So we must put a 2 in row 3. That leaves the 1 in row 3, column 3. Finishing up column 2, we know that row 2 is a 7 or 6. The only way to reach 26 is 2+9+8+7. So we must put a 7 in row 2. We put the remaining 6 in row 2 column 3.

Finishing column 2, we know the top and bottom digits must be 9 and 8, in some order. If we place the 9 in the bottom row, then we would have to place a 6 into column 3; however, there already is a 6 there in row 2. Thus, we place the 9 in the top row and the 8 in the bottom row. We then easily complete the remainder of the puzzle.

Magnets Example

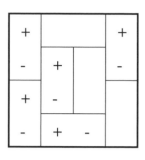

In our Magnets puzzles, we have to place some magnets into the grid. Each magnet consists of a positive and a negative pole. Similar to real magnets, two magnets cannot have the same kind of pole adjacent to each other (meaning you cannot have two + or two – adjacent to one another). Clues outside the grid correspond to the number of + or – in that row or column. Note that some rows and columns may not have number clues.

To start filling this in, let's look at the top row. We see there are two + and no – in that row. This means we can't place any magnet into the horizontal spot, and so the two boxes in columns 1 and 4 must contain magnets, with the positive pole in row 1 and the negative poles in row 2.

Looking now at column 2, our clue tells us we must have 2 positive poles and 1 negative pole. Since column 1, row 2 is negative, column 2, row 2 must be a positive, with its negative directly below it. The final positive is in row 4, column 2, with its negative pole next to it in column 3.

Finally, we look at row 4. The clue tells us it has 1 positive pole and 2 negative poles. The only place we can put the other magnet is in column 1, with the – in row 4, and the + in row 3.

Looking at the grid, one might wonder if a magnet can be placed into the box in the middle of column 3, as there are no clues pointing to it. We see that the cell in row 2 has two different poles adjacent to it: the + in column 2, and the – in column 4. No matter what magnet we place into that cell, that would violate the rule of having two adjacent poles. As a result, that box must remain empty, and we have completed the puzzle!

Mastermind Example

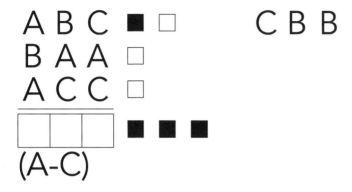

(A-C)

In the Mastermind puzzles featured in this book, you must find the correct three-letter combination of the letters A, B, and C. Letters may be repeated in the correct answer, and the letters may be in any order.

In this example, three incorrect combinations have been listed to get you started; those combinations come with at least one of two types of clues to help you. A black square next to a combination indicates that one of the letters in the combination is in the correct spot. A white square indicates that there is a correct letter in the combination, but it is not in the right spot.

Consider the first combination given. The black square means that one letter is in the correct place; the white square means that another is in the correct answer, but not in the right place. In the second combination given, the white square means only one of A and B are in the correct answer, but not both, and we know it is not in the right spot. Combining the two, we know that C must be in the puzzle.

Looking at the third combination, we know that C must not be the second or third letter, otherwise we would have a black square as a clue. So C is our correct first letter. We also know that A is not in the correct answer, otherwise we would have had two white squares in the third row clue. So C is our first letter, and B is the other two.

Mintonette Example

 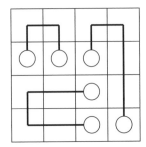

In the Mintonette puzzles, we must connect all circles in pairs in the grid. There are two basic rules: (1) The connecting path between two circles must turn exactly twice. (2) When we are done, all the cells in the grid must be used. Based on these rules, there's exactly one way to draw all the paths.

To start, let's look at the circle in the bottom right corner. The only way we can make a path that turns twice is drawing the line all the way up that column and turn left into row 3. We don't know yet which circle it will pair with, but any other path would connect with another circle without taking exactly 2 turns.

Now let's look at the top left corner of the grid. It does not contain a circle, but must be part of a path. Thus, its path must originate at the circle below it, moving up and then left. So our grid looks like:

Looking at the bottom two cells in column 1, both are now corners, so must connect to each other.

As the path involving these cells has two turns already, they both must extend to the nearest circles. Finally, the circles in row 2 that have no path yet must both have their paths go up, completing the puzzle.

Sudoku Example

				1	2
3					
			4	5	
	4	1			
					6
4	2				

6	5	4	3	1	2
3	1	2	5	6	4
2	6	3	4	5	1
5	4	1	6	2	3
1	3	5	2	4	6
4	2	6	1	3	5

Sudoku has become a popular puzzle around the world. Place numbers into the grid so that each row, column, and bold outlined box has the digits, in this example, from 1–6 (although puzzles may go up to 9). Digits cannot repeat in a row, column, or bold outlined box.

To start in this example, we can look in row 1. Where can we place the 3? It can't be in the first three columns, as those share the box with the 3 in row 2. Thus, we can place the 3 in row 1, column 4 (R1C4 for short). Similarly, for the 1 in row 2, we can't place it in columns 4–6 (shares a box with the 1 in R1C5), nor can we place it in column 3 (shares the column with the 1 in R4C3). Therefore, we place the 1 in R2C2 and a 2 in R2C3. Similar logic places digits in R3C6, R4C1, R5C4, R5C5, and R6C3.

If we look at column 5, we know that the digits in rows 2, 4, and 6 are 2/3/6 in some order. Looking at the bottom right box, we see 2 and 6 are already in the box. This allows us to place 3 in R6C5, then 6 in R2C5, and 2 in R4C5. We can then complete the right-hand side of the puzzle, and use similar logic to fill in the left side of the grid to complete the solution.

Puzzles

Sudoku 1

Enter all the digits from 1–9 in each box, such that no digit repeats in each row, column, or box.

1		4				6		5
	2			8			3	
5		3				4		2
			9		8			
2	6			7			5	4
			6		5			
3		7				5		8
	4			5			6	
6		5				9		7

Sudoku 2

Enter all the digits from 1–9 in each box, such that no digit repeats in each row, column, or box.

4				1				2
	5		2		3		1	
		3				5		
	2			8			7	
1			4		2			9
	3			6			8	
		5				7		
	8		7		6		3	
7				5				6

Sudoku 3

Enter all the digits from 1–9 in each box, such that no digit repeats in each row, column, or box.

8			5		2			9
	4			3			5	
		6		4		1		
		2		3				
	1	2				5	6	
		7		6				
		3		7		2		
	9			8			4	
1			3		4			6

Sudoku 4

Enter all the digits from 1–9 in each box, such that no digit repeats in each row, column, or box.

		3			1			9
	2			4			7	
1			7			8		
		6			2			7
	5			8			1	
4			5			6		
		9			3			1
	8			9			6	
7			6			4		

Sudoku 5

Enter all the digits from 1–9 in each box, such that no digit repeats in each row, column, or box.

		3			1			8
	2			4			3	
1			7			2		
		6			2			5
	5			8			2	
4			5			8		
		9			3			1
	8			9			6	
7			6			4		

Sudoku 6

Enter all the digits from 1–9 in each box, such that no digit repeats in each row, column, or box.

	1	2	3					
4				5				
6								
7							4	6
8		3	2			5		1
9				6			7	2
1				8				9
2				7				3
	4	5	6			1	8	

Sudoku 7

Enter all the digits from 1–9 in each box, such that no digit repeats in each row, column, or box.

1		3			8		5	4
2		4				3		
	9						7	8
7				6				
			5	7	9			
				8				5
3	4						2	
		1				9		6
5	6		4			8		7

Sudoku 8

Enter all the digits from 1–9 in each box, such that no digit repeats in each row, column, or box.

							5	
		3			6		8	
1		4			2		7	
2		5			1			
3		6			7	8	2	
4		8						
5		2	4	6	8	7	1	
6								
7	8	9	1	3	5	6		

Sudoku 9

Enter all the digits from 1–9 in each box, such that no digit repeats in each row, column, or box.

		3		5		7		
	2		4		6		8	
1								9
	9						4	
3			8	4	2			6
	4						2	
6								1
	5		2		7		3	
		4		9		5		

Sudoku 10

Enter all the digits from 1–9 in each box, such that no digit repeats in each row, column, or box.

	6	5				2	4	
2			4					5
7				3				6
				2			5	
		6	3	1	5	8		
	7			4				
8				5				9
9					6			1
	5	1				7	8	

Sudoku 11

Enter all the digits from 1–9 in each box, such that no digit repeats in each row, column, or box.

	4	3	2					
5				1				
6							2	3
	7					4		
		8				5	6	9
			9					7
				9		7	3	
1				8				
	3	5	7					

Sudoku 12

Enter all the digits from 1–9 in each box, such that no digit repeats in each row, column, or box.

6				7				4
		1				5		
	8	2	3	4	5	6	9	
		3				7		
1		4				8		6
		5				9		
	1	6	7	8	9	3	2	
		7				4		
9				2				7

Mastermind 3

Someone has created a hidden password, and it is up to you to try to crack it! Four incorrect guesses have been made, and you now have some information about the password. A black square next to the guess states that a letter in the password is in its correct spot. A white square next to the guess indicates that there is a letter that is in the password, but it's not in the right spot. Below the puzzle is the range of letters allowed to be used in the password. Using the guesses, can you crack the password?

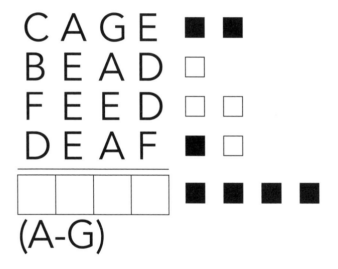

(A-G)

Mastermind 4

Someone has created a hidden password, and it is up to you to try to crack it! Seven incorrect guesses have been made, and you now have some information about the password. A black square next to the guess states that a letter in the password is in its correct spot. A white square next to the guess indicates that there is a letter that is in the password, but it's not in the right spot. Below the puzzle is the range of letters allowed to be used in the password. Using the guesses, can you crack the password?

EAGLE　□ □ □

ESSAY　■ □

ENTER　■ □

ETHIC　□ □

EARLY　□ □ □ □

EERIE　□ □

ELECT　■ ■ □

□□□□□　■ ■ ■ ■ ■

(A-Z)

Mastermind 5

Someone has created a hidden password, and it is up to you to try to crack it! Five incorrect guesses have been made, and you now have some information about the password. A black square next to the guess states that a letter in the password is in its correct spot. A white square next to the guess indicates that there is a letter that is in the password, but it's not in the right spot. Below the puzzle is the range of letters allowed to be used in the password. Using the guesses, can you crack the password?

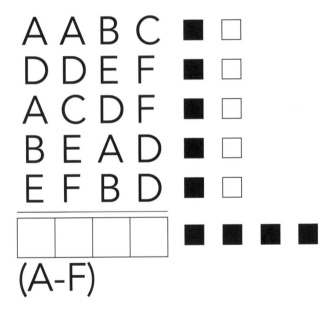

Mastermind 6

Someone has created a hidden password, and it is up to you to try to crack it! Seven incorrect guesses have been made, and you now have some information about the password. A black square next to the guess states that a letter in the password is in its correct spot. A white square next to the guess indicates that there is a letter that is in the password, but it's not in the right spot. Below the puzzle is the range of letters allowed to be used in the password. Using the guesses, can you crack the password?

(A-M)

Mastermind 7

Someone has created a hidden password, and it is up to you to try to crack it! Three incorrect guesses have been made, and you now have some information about the password. A black square next to the guess states that a letter in the password is in its correct spot. A white square next to the guess indicates that there is a letter that is in the password, but it's not in the right spot. Below the puzzle is the range of letters allowed to be used in the password. Using the guesses, can you crack the password?

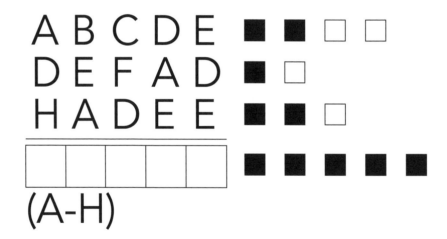

(A-H)

Mastermind 8

Someone has created a hidden password, and it is up to you to try to crack it! Four incorrect guesses have been made, and you now have some information about the password. A black square next to the guess states that a letter in the password is in its correct spot. A white square next to the guess indicates that there is a letter that is in the password, but it's not in the right spot. Below the puzzle is the range of letters allowed to be used in the password. Using the guesses, can you crack the password?

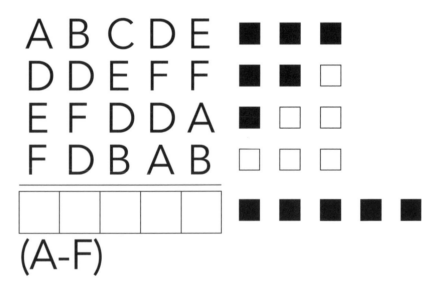

(A-F)

Mastermind 9

Someone has created a hidden password, and it is up to you to try to crack it! Four incorrect guesses have been made, and you now have some information about the password. A black square next to the guess states that a letter in the password is in its correct spot. A white square next to the guess indicates that there is a letter that is in the password, but it's not in the right spot. Below the puzzle is the range of letters allowed to be used in the password. Using the guesses, can you crack the password?

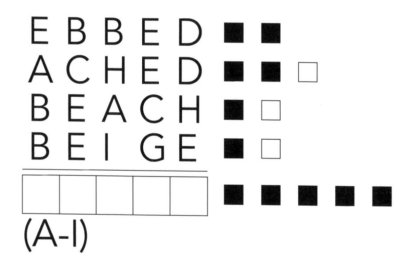

(A-I)

Mastermind 10

Someone has created a hidden password, and it is up to you to try to crack it! Five incorrect guesses have been made, and you now have some information about the password. A black square next to the guess states that a letter in the password is in its correct spot. A white square next to the guess indicates that there is a letter that is in the password, but it's not in the right spot. Below the puzzle is the range of letters allowed to be used in the password. Using the guesses, can you crack the password?

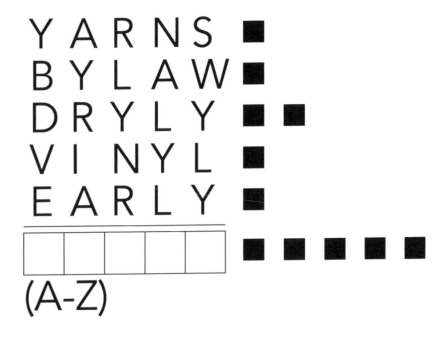

Y A R N S ■
B Y L A W ■
D R Y L Y ■ ■
V I N Y L ■
E A R L Y ■

(A-Z)

Mastermind 11

Someone has created a hidden password, and it is up to you to try to crack it! Five incorrect guesses have been made, and you now have some information about the password. A black square next to the guess states that a letter in the password is in its correct spot. A white square next to the guess indicates that there is a letter that is in the password, but it's not in the right spot. Below the puzzle is the range of letters allowed to be used in the password. Using the guesses, can you crack the password?

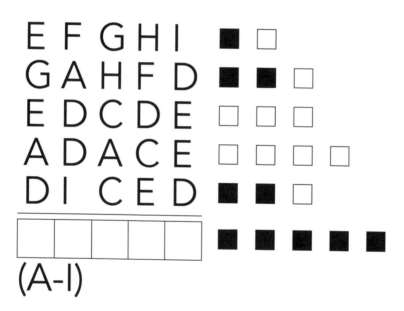

(A-I)

Fill-In 1

Place each given word once into the grid, filling it out crossword style.

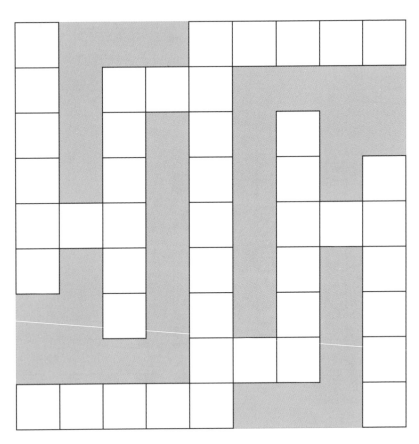

END	TOMES	OFFICE
FAR	TOWER	WINDOW
NEE	BROKEN	TRASHCANS
WAR	CRANKS	

Fill-In 2

Place each given word once into the grid, filling it out crossword style.

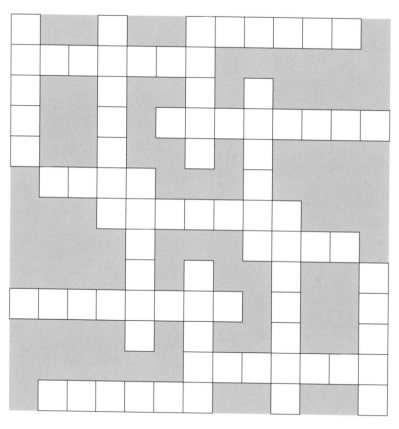

CRAB	SWISH	GRUNION	FLOUNDER
GRUB	BELUGA	LEAKING	STINGRAY
GATOR	DUGONG	MANATEE	
SEALS	OYSTER	NARWHAL	
SMELT	SPONGE	OCTOPUS	

Fill-In 3

Place each given word once into the grid, filling it out crossword style.

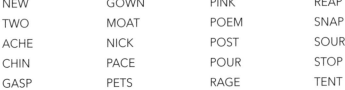

NEW	GOWN	PINK	REAP
TWO	MOAT	POEM	SNAP
ACHE	NICK	POST	SOUR
CHIN	PACE	POUR	STOP
GASP	PETS	RAGE	TENT

Fill-In 4

Place each given word once into the grid, filling it out crossword style.

CHASM	FIRST	OTTER	SONIC
DELTA	KOALA	RADII	TABOO
DREAM	LARVA	RAKED	TOTES
EBBED	LIMIT	ROMEO	TRAIL
FILET	NERVE	SALAD	TROTS

Fill-In 5

Place each given word once into the grid, filling it out crossword style.

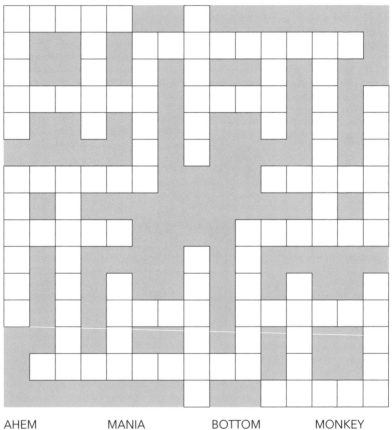

AHEM	MANIA	BOTTOM	MONKEY
LIME	MESSY	EMBLEM	IMMATURE
MATH	MODEM	IMPORT	SMALLEST
OVUM	NAMES	LIMBER	LIMITLESS
EMPTY	SMELL	LIMBIC	MECHANICS
IDIOM	BEDLAM	MADAME	
IMPLY	BLAMES	MAILER	

Fill-In 6

Place each given word once into the grid, filling it out crossword style.

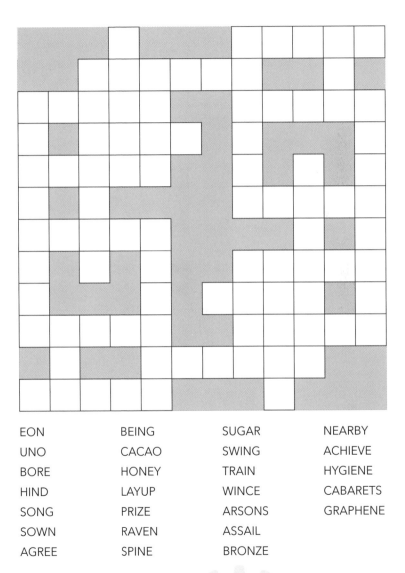

EON	BEING	SUGAR	NEARBY
UNO	CACAO	SWING	ACHIEVE
BORE	HONEY	TRAIN	HYGIENE
HIND	LAYUP	WINCE	CABARETS
SONG	PRIZE	ARSONS	GRAPHENE
SOWN	RAVEN	ASSAIL	
AGREE	SPINE	BRONZE	

Fill-In 7

Place each given word once into the grid, filling it out crossword style.

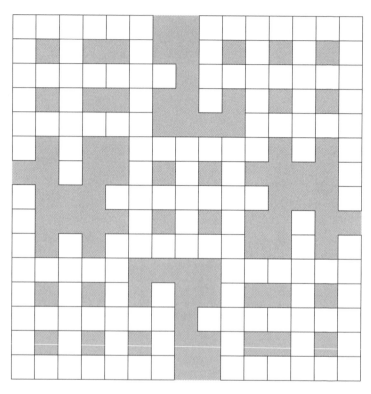

CORN	SAINTS	URCHIN	SCOURED
TROD	SISTER	ATHLETE	SIBLING
NOVEL	STRESS	BARBELL	CARPORTS
PASTA	TENORS	BRAVEST	CASTANET
RUMBA	THERMO	CAUSTIC	RAINSTORMS
ASIAGO	TOKENS	REACTOR	RESTAURANT
PASTOR	ULCERS	ROBOTIC	
PSYLLA	UNCLES	ROCKETS	

Fill-In 8

Place each given word once into the grid, filling it out crossword style.

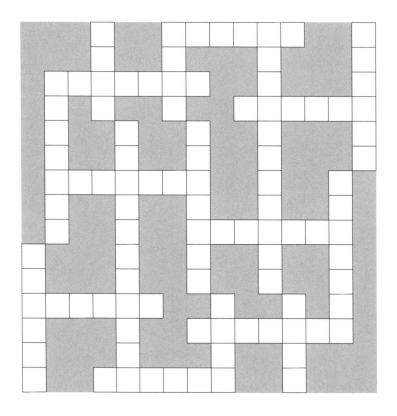

URNS	UNBIND	UGLIEST	UNUSUAL
URUS	UNPLUG	UMLAUTS	USHERED
USED	UPDATE	UMPIRES	UNAMBIGUITY
UTAH	URGENT	UNSOUND	UNIFICATION
UMBRAE	USURPS	UNTRIED	

Fill-In 9

Place each given word once into the grid, filling it out crossword style.

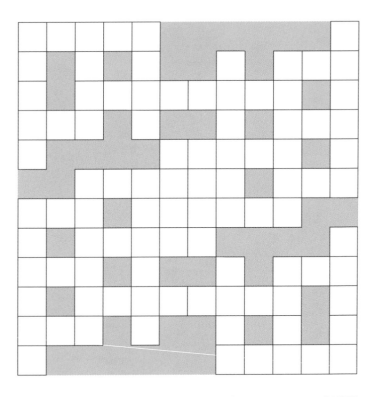

ADO	AGAR	FROWN	HOUSES
AIR	DIRE	GAVEL	MINERS
BEE	LAPS	GOURD	ORDERS
DUO	NOUN	SNEAK	SECOND
END	SHOW	AFFORD	ROUNDING
OFF	VASE	ANCHOR	SUPERIOR
ROD	DRIED	BRAKES	
ROE	ERRED	CHORUS	

Fill-In 10

Place each given word once into the grid, filling it out crossword style.

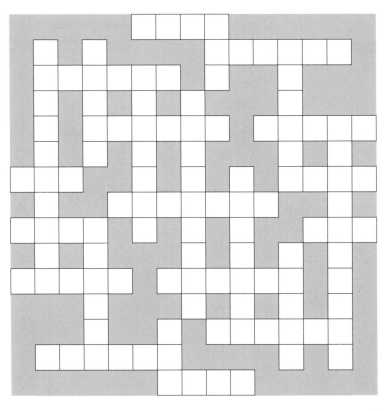

ASK	HEART	OPAQUE	VIRTUELESS
BLAZE	IMPRESSIVE	PTOSIS	WAIL
COPIOUS	JUMPING	QUARRY	XYLOPHONE
DROVE	KATANA	RIFF	YARD
ENAMEL	LOW	SUN	ZEPHYR
FOREST	MALICE	TAN	
GLASS	NOUN	UNKEMPT	

Catwalk 1

Draw a path from the cat to its milk bowl; each step in the path will move either horizontally or vertically, and will never revisit a previously visited cell. Clues outside the grid indicate the number of cells that the cat's path visits in the row or column.

Catwalk 2

Draw a path from the cat to its milk bowl; each step in the path will move either horizontally or vertically, and will never revisit a previously visited cell. Clues outside the grid indicate the number of cells that the cat's path visits in the row or column.

Catwalk 3

Draw a path from the cat to its milk bowl; each step in the path will move either horizontally or vertically, and will never revisit a previously visited cell. Clues outside the grid indicate the number of cells that the cat's path visits in the row or column.

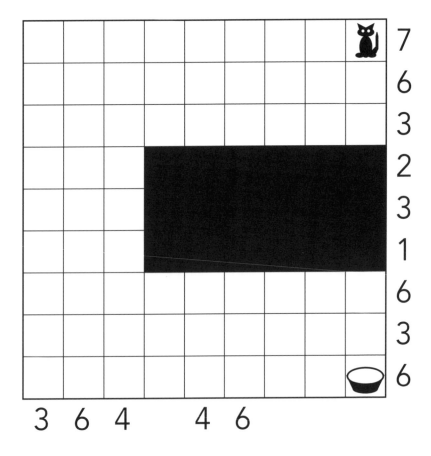

Catwalk 4

Draw a path from the cat to its milk bowl; each step in the path will move either horizontally or vertically, and will never revisit a previously visited cell. Clues outside the grid indicate the number of cells that the cat's path visits in the row or column. In this puzzle, some clues have been omitted.

Catwalk 5

Draw a path from the cat to its milk bowl; each step in the path will move either horizontally or vertically, and will never revisit a previously visited cell. Clues outside the grid indicate the number of cells that the cat's path visits in the row or column. In this puzzle, some clues have been omitted.

3 1 4 1 5

Catwalk 6

Draw a path from the cat to its milk bowl; each step in the path will move either horizontally or vertically, and will never revisit a previously visited cell. Clues outside the grid indicate the number of cells that the cat's path visits in the row or column. In this puzzle, some clues have been omitted.

Catwalk 7

Draw a path from the cat to its milk bowl; each step in the path will move either horizontally or vertically, and will never revisit a previously visited cell. Clues outside the grid indicate the number of cells that the cat's path visits in the row or column. In this puzzle, multiple cats and bowls are present; determining which bowl belongs to which cat is a part of the puzzle.

Catwalk 8

Draw a path from the cat to its milk bowl; each step in the path will move either horizontally or vertically, and will never revisit a previously visited cell. Clues outside the grid indicate the number of cells that the cat's path visits in the row or column. In this puzzle, some clues have been omitted.

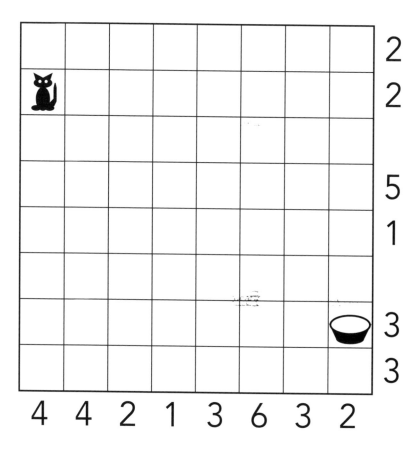

Catwalk 9

Draw a path from the cat to its milk bowl; each step in the path will move either horizontally or vertically, and will never revisit a previously visited cell. Clues outside the grid indicate the number of cells that the cat's path visits in the row or column. In this puzzle, some clues have been omitted. Also, multiple cats and bowls are present; determining which bowl belongs to which cat is a part of the puzzle.

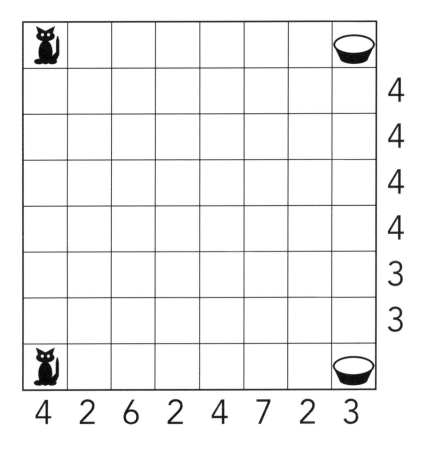

Catwalk 10

Draw a path from the cat to its milk bowl; each step in the path will move either horizontally or vertically, and will never revisit a previously visited cell. Clues outside the grid indicate the number of cells that the cat's path visits in the row or column. In this puzzle, some clues have been omitted. Also, multiple cats and bowls are present; determining which bowl belongs to which cat is a part of the puzzle.

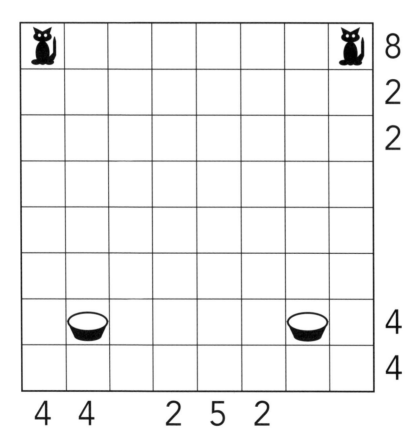

Catwalk 11

Draw a path from each cat to its milk bowl; each step in the path will move either horizontally or vertically, and will never revisit a previously visited cell. Clues outside the grid indicate the number of cells that a cat's path visits in the row or column. In this puzzle, some clues have been omitted. Also, multiple cats and bowls are present; determining which bowl belongs to which cat is part of the puzzle.

Catwalk 12

Draw a path from the cat to its milk bowl; each step in the path will move either horizontally or vertically, and will never revisit a previously visited cell. Clues outside the grid indicate the number of cells that the cat's path visits in the row or column. In this puzzle, some clues have been omitted. Also, multiple cats and bowls are present; determining which bowl belongs to which cat is a part of the puzzle.

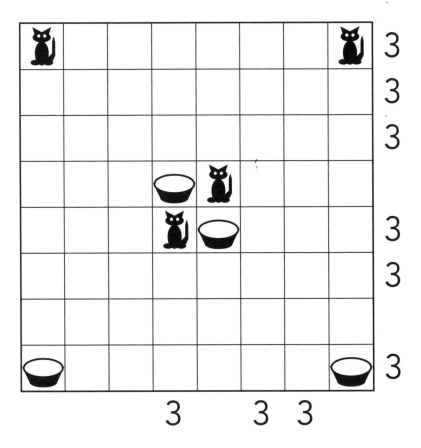

Catwalk 13

Draw a path from the cat to its milk bowl; each step in the path will move either horizontally or vertically, and will never revisit a previously visited cell. Clues outside the grid indicate the number of cells that the cat's path visits in the row or column. In this puzzle, some clues have been omitted.

Easy as ABC 1

Place letters, which in this puzzle are A–E, into the grid such that each letter appears once in each row and column. Cells may remain blank, and no two digits may touch each other horizontally, vertically, or diagonally. Letters outside the grid indicate the first letter seen from that direction.

Easy as ABC 2

Place letters, which in this puzzle are A–C, into the grid such that each letter appears once in each row and column. Cells may remain blank, and no two digits may touch each other horizontally, vertically, or diagonally. Letters outside the grid indicate the first letter seen from that direction.

Easy as ABC 3

Place letters, which in this puzzle are A–D, into the grid such that each letter appears once in each row and column. Cells may remain blank, and no two digits may touch each other horizontally, vertically, or diagonally. Letters outside the grid indicate the first letter seen from that direction.

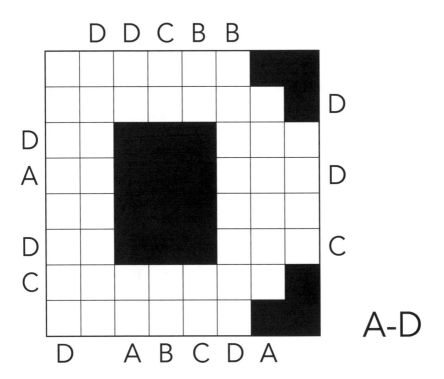

Easy as ABC 4

Place letters, which in this puzzle are A–C, into the grid such that each letter appears once in each row and column. Cells may remain blank, and no two digits may touch each other horizontally, vertically, or diagonally. Letters outside the grid indicate the first letter seen from that direction.

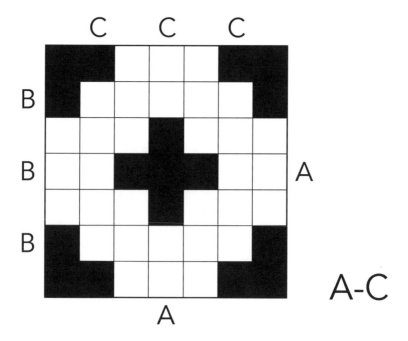

Easy as ABC 5

Place letters, which in this puzzle are A–D, into the grid such that each letter appears once in each row and column. Cells may remain blank, and no two digits may touch each other horizontally, vertically, or diagonally. Letters outside the grid indicate the first letter seen from that direction.

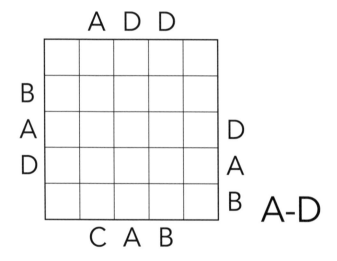

Easy as ABC 6

Place letters, which in this puzzle are A–C, into the grid such that each letter appears once in each row and column. Cells may remain blank, and no two digits may touch each other horizontally, vertically, or diagonally. Letters outside the grid indicate the first letter seen from that direction.

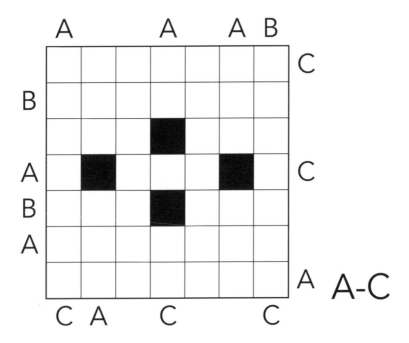

Easy as ABC 7

Place letters, which in this puzzle are A–C, into the grid such that each letter appears once in each row and column. Cells may remain blank, and no two digits may touch each other horizontally, vertically, or diagonally. Letters outside the grid indicate the first letter seen from that direction.

Easy as ABC 8

Place letters, which in this puzzle are A–C, into the grid such that each letter appears once in each row and column. Cells may remain blank, and no two digits may touch each other horizontally, vertically, or diagonally. Letters outside the grid indicate the first letter seen from that direction.

Easy as ABC 9

Place letters, which in this puzzle are A–D, into the grid such that each letter appears once in each row and column. Cells may remain blank, and no two digits may touch each other horizontally, vertically, or diagonally. Letters outside the grid indicate the first letter seen from that direction.

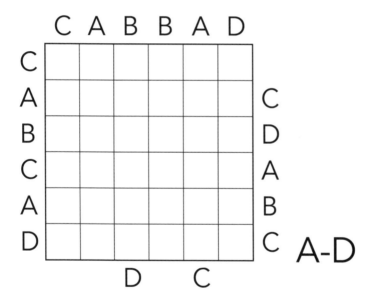

Grades 1

Place single-digit numbers into the grid. A box with a number cannot touch another box with a number either horizontally, vertically, or diagonally. That means some cells will be left blank. Above and to the left of the grid, the given clues tell us how many numbers are in each column or row. The bottom and right clues correspond to the sum of the numbers in that column or row.

Grades 2

Place single-digit numbers into the grid. A box with a number cannot touch another box with a number either horizontally, vertically, or diagonally. That means some cells will be left blank. Above and to the left of the grid, the given clues tell us how many numbers are in each column or row. The bottom and right clues correspond to the sum of the numbers in that column or row.

Grades 3

Place single-digit numbers into the grid. A box with a number cannot touch another box with a number either horizontally, vertically, or diagonally. That means some cells will be left blank. Above and to the left of the grid, the given clues tell us how many numbers are in each column or row. The bottom and right clues correspond to the sum of the numbers in that column or row.

Grades 4

Place single-digit numbers into the grid. A box with a number cannot touch another box with a number either horizontally, vertically, or diagonally. That means some cells will be left blank. Above and to the left of the grid, the given clues tell us how many numbers are in each column or row. The bottom and right clues correspond to the sum of the numbers in that column or row.

Grades 5

Place single-digit numbers into the grid. A box with a number cannot touch another box with a number either horizontally, vertically, or diagonally. That means some cells will be left blank. Above and to the left of the grid, the given clues tell us how many numbers are in each column or row. The bottom and right clues correspond to the sum of the numbers in that column or row.

	3	1	2	1	2	2	2	1	
2									8
1									8
3									8
1									8
2									8
2									8
1									8
2									8
	13	8	9	5	7	6	15	1	

Grades 6

Place single-digit numbers into the grid. A box with a number cannot touch another box with a number either horizontally, vertically, or diagonally. That means some cells will be left blank. Above and to the left of the grid, the given clues tell us how many numbers are in each column or row. The bottom and right clues correspond to the sum of the numbers in that column or row. In this puzzle, some of the clues have been omitted and you must solve the puzzle without them.

Grades 7

Place single-digit numbers into the grid. A box with a number cannot touch another box with a number either horizontally, vertically, or diagonally. That means some cells will be left blank. Above and to the left of the grid, the given clues tell us how many numbers are in each column or row. The bottom and right clues correspond to the sum of the numbers in that column or row.

	2	1	1	2	1	1	2	1	
1									8
2									13
1									2
1									4
2									8
1									1
1									9
2									10
	7	3	5	10	9	4	14	3	

Grades 8

Place single-digit numbers into the grid. A box with a number cannot touch another box with a number either horizontally, vertically, or diagonally. That means some cells will be left blank. Above and to the left of the grid, the given clues tell us how many numbers are in each column or row. The bottom and right clues correspond to the sum of the numbers in that column or row.

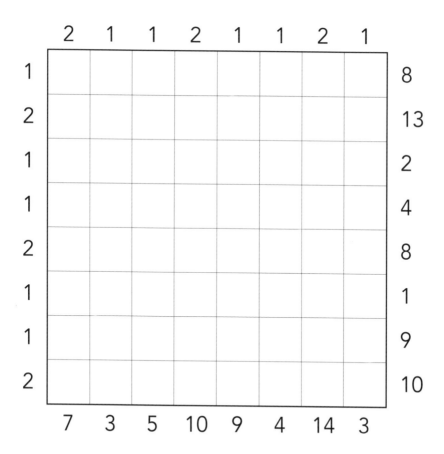

	2	1	1	2	1	1	2	1	
1									8
2									13
1									2
1									4
2									8
1									1
1									9
2									10
	7	3	5	10	9	4	14	3	

Grades 9

Place single-digit numbers into the grid. A box with a number cannot touch another box with a number either horizontally, vertically, or diagonally. That means some cells will be left blank. Above and to the left of the grid, the given clues tell us how many numbers are in each column or row. The bottom and right clues correspond to the sum of the numbers in that column or row.

	1	2	1	3	1	3	1	2	
3									7
1									5
2									14
1									4
2									9
1									8
2									12
2									2
	6	12	4	11	9	8	5	6	

Grades 10

Place single-digit numbers into the grid. A box with a number cannot touch another box with a number either horizontally, vertically, or diagonally. That means some cells will be left blank. Above and to the left of the grid, the given clues tell us how many numbers are in each column or row. The bottom and right clues correspond to the sum of the numbers in that column or row. In this puzzle, some of the clues have been omitted and you must solve the puzzle without them.

Grades 11

Place single-digit numbers into the grid. A box with a number cannot touch another box with a number either horizontally, vertically, or diagonally. That means some cells will be left blank. Above and to the left of the grid, the given clues tell us how many numbers are in each column or row. The bottom and right clues correspond to the sum of the numbers in that column or row. In this puzzle, some of the clues have been omitted and you must solve the puzzle without them.

Grades 12

Place single-digit numbers into the grid. A box with a number cannot touch another box with a number either horizontally, vertically, or diagonally. That means some cells will be left blank. Above and to the left of the grid, the given clues tell us how many numbers are in each column or row. The bottom and right clues correspond to the sum of the numbers in that column or row.

	2	2	1	1	2	1	2	2	
2									13
2									7
1									8
2									10
1									4
2									7
1									2
2									14
	9	16	7	1	5	4	15	8	

Grades 13

Place single-digit numbers into the grid. A box with a number cannot touch another box with a number either horizontally, vertically, or diagonally. That means some cells will be left blank. Above and to the left of the grid, the given clues tell us how many numbers are in each column or row. The bottom and right clues correspond to the sum of the numbers in that column or row. In this puzzle, some of the clues have been omitted and you must solve the puzzle without them.

Kakuro 1

Place a digit from 1–9 in each cell. The number above a diagonal line tells the sum of the digits in the cells immediately to its right. The number below the diagonal tells the sum of the cells immediately below it. Digits cannot repeat within a sum.

Kakuro 2

Place a digit from 1–9 in each cell. The number above a diagonal line tells the sum of the digits in the cells immediately to its right. The number below the diagonal tells the sum of the cells immediately below it. Digits cannot repeat within a sum.

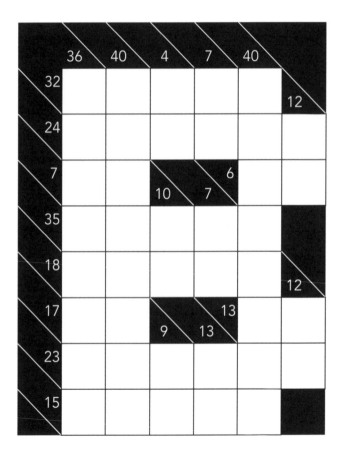

Kakuro 3

Place a digit from 1–9 in each cell. The number above a diagonal line tells the sum of the digits in the cells immediately to its right. The number below the diagonal tells the sum of the cells immediately below it. Digits cannot repeat within a sum.

Kakuro 4

Place a digit from 1–9 in each cell. The number above a diagonal line tells the sum of the digits in the cells immediately to its right. The number below the diagonal tells the sum of the cells immediately below it. Digits cannot repeat within a sum.

Kakuro 5

Place a digit from 1–9 in each cell. The number above a diagonal line tells the sum of the digits in the cells immediately to its right. The number below the diagonal tells the sum of the cells immediately below it. Digits cannot repeat within a sum.

Kakuro 6

Place a digit from 1–9 in each cell. The number above a diagonal line tells the sum of the digits in the cells immediately to its right. The number below the diagonal tells the sum of the cells immediately below it. Digits cannot repeat within a sum.

Kakuro 7

Place a digit from 1–9 in each cell. The number above a diagonal line tells the sum of the digits in the cells immediately to its right. The number below the diagonal tells the sum of the cells immediately below it. Digits cannot repeat within a sum.

Kakuro 8

Place a digit from 1–9 in each cell. The number above a diagonal line tells the sum of the digits in the cells immediately to its right. The number below the diagonal tells the sum of the cells immediately below it. Digits cannot repeat within a sum.

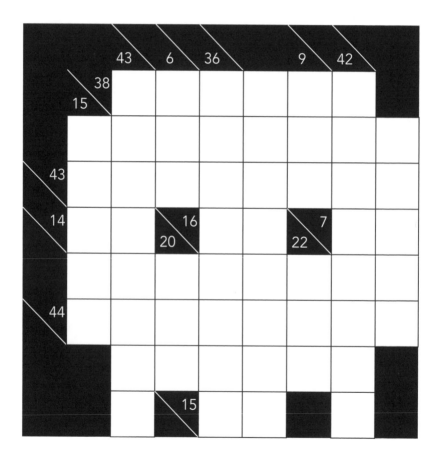

Kakuro 9

Place a digit from 1–9 in each cell. The number above a diagonal line tells the sum of the digits in the cells immediately to its right. The number below the diagonal tells the sum of the cells immediately below it. Digits cannot repeat within a sum.

Magnets 1

Place magnets into the diagram; some of the boxes will contain magnets, and some will remain empty. Each magnet has a positive and negative pole, and adjacent cells cannot contain the same pole. The number of positive and negative poles in each row are given; in some puzzles, some of these numbers may be omitted.

				2	3
				2	2
				2	1
				1	1
				2	2
				1	1

2	1	2	2	1	+
1	2	2	1	2	-

Magnets 2

Place magnets into the diagram; some of the boxes will contain magnets, and some will remain empty. Each magnet has a positive and negative pole, and adjacent cells cannot contain the same pole. The number of positive and negative poles in each row are given; in some puzzles, some of these numbers may be omitted.

						+	-
						2	1
						1	1
						3	2
						1	3
						1	2
						2	1
2	2	2	1	1	2	+	
2	3	1	1	1	2	-	

Magnets 3

Place magnets into the diagram; some of the boxes will contain magnets, and some will remain empty. Each magnet has a positive and negative pole, and adjacent cells cannot contain the same pole. The number of positive and negative poles in each row are given; in some puzzles, some of these numbers may be omitted.

Magnets 4

Place magnets into the diagram; some of the boxes will contain magnets, and some will remain empty. Each magnet has a positive and negative pole, and adjacent cells cannot contain the same pole. The number of positive and negative poles in each row are given; in some puzzles, some of these numbers may be omitted.

						3	3
						2	1
						3	2
						2	4
						2	4
						2	2
						3	2

2 3 2 3   2 3   +

3 3 2 3   2 3   −

Magnets 5

Place magnets into the diagram; some of the boxes will contain magnets, and some will remain empty. Each magnet has a positive and negative pole, and adjacent cells cannot contain the same pole. The number of positive and negative poles in each row are given; in some puzzles, some of these numbers may be omitted.

			3	1
2	3
1	3
3	3
3	3
3	1

| 3 | 2 | | 2 | 3 | | 2 | 1 | + |
| 3 | 3 | | 3 | 2 | | 2 | 2 | - |

Magnets 6

Place magnets into the diagram; some of the boxes will contain magnets, and some will remain empty. Each magnet has a positive and negative pole, and adjacent cells cannot contain the same pole. The number of positive and negative poles in each row are given; in some puzzles, some of these numbers may be omitted.

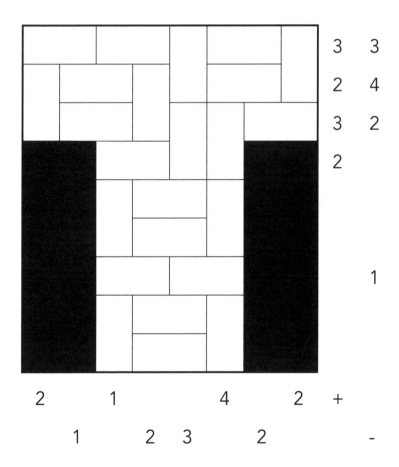

Magnets 7

Place magnets into the diagram; some of the boxes will contain magnets, and some will remain empty. Each magnet has a positive and negative pole, and adjacent cells cannot contain the same pole. The number of positive and negative poles in each row are given; in some puzzles, some of these numbers may be omitted.

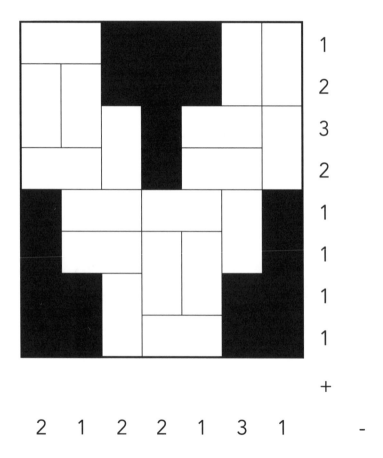

Magnets 8

Place magnets into the diagram; some of the boxes will contain magnets, and some will remain empty. Each magnet has a positive and negative pole, and adjacent cells cannot contain the same pole. The number of positive and negative poles in each row are given; in some puzzles, some of these numbers may be omitted.

										+	-
										5	3
										1	2
										3	3
										4	4
										1	3
										3	2
										2	1
										4	4
										2	3
										3	3
3	2	3	4	2	3	3	2	2	4	+	
3	3	4	1	3	2	3	1	4	4	-	

Mintonette 1

The circles are connected in pairs by lines. Each line makes exactly 2 turns between the circles. All cells in the grid are used by the lines.

Mintonette 2

The circles are connected in pairs by lines. Each line makes exactly 2 turns between the circles. All cells in the grid are used by the lines.

Mintonette 3

The circles are connected in pairs by lines. Each line makes exactly 2 turns between the circles. All cells in the grid are used by the lines.

Mintonette 4

The circles are connected in pairs by lines. Each line makes exactly 2 turns between the circles. All cells in the grid are used by the lines.

Mintonette 5

The circles are connected in pairs by lines. Each line makes exactly
2 turns between the circles. All cells in the grid are used by the lines.

Mintonette 6

The circles are connected in pairs by lines. Unlike previous Mintonette
puzzles, this variation requires 3 turns between each circle, instead of 2.
All cells in the grid are used by the lines.

Mintonette 7

The circles are connected in pairs by lines. Unlike previous Mintonette puzzles, this variation requires 3 turns between each circle, instead of 2. All cells in the grid are used by the lines.

Mintonette 8

The circles are connected in pairs by lines. Unlike previous Mintonette puzzles, this variation requires 3 turns between each circle, instead of 2. All cells in the grid are used by the lines.

Word Search 1

Find these uplifting words in the grid.

```
R T I C K L E D P I N K E C L
D C A P H L U F Y A L P W H N
P E L H L I V E L Y Y D A I I
I I T A E B P U N P I E L R L
J R I A E T Y P P A H U K P N
U U L I L N L E E I F P I Y D
B S A L G E P A I R U H N D E
I C I T A T S C E D L O G E Y
L O N S J N A E A H U R O T O
A R E C L O H F F O F I N H J
N D G H U C L U C K Y C A G R
T I N D T T I L D U O R I I E
N A C K H I P A Y D J O R L V
A L T O N C L O U D N I N E O
S U N N Y G E B L E S S E D M
```

BLESSED	ECSTATIC	JOYFUL	PEPPY
BLITHE	ELATED	JUBILANT	PLAYFUL
CHEERFUL	EUPHORIC	LIVELY	PLEASED
CHIPPER	GENIAL	LUCKY	SUNNY
CHIRPY	GLAD	MERRY	TICKLED PINK
CONTENT	GLEE	ON CLOUD NINE	UPBEAT
CORDIAL	HAPPY	OVERJOYED	WALKING ON AIR
DELIGHTED	JOLLY	PEACEFUL	

Word Search 2

If you're feeling musical, find these composers hidden in the grid below.

```
U  O  S  I  D  L  A  V  I  V  R  A  V  E  L
H  H  T  R  T  R  E  B  U  H  C  S  H  N  D
I  Y  R  S  S  U  I  L  E  B  I  S  S  L  B
Y  K  A  V  H  Z  R  E  L  H  A  M  E  Y  E
L  S  U  H  E  O  E  Z  S  S  H  I  C  K  E
E  G  S  T  L  I  S  Z  T  A  F  O  C  S  T
D  R  S  U  L  L  S  T  R  A  Z  O  M  V  H
N  O  S  N  B  R  A  B  A  C  H  N  V  O  O
A  S  G  H  H  E  H  D  V  K  D  R  E  K  V
H  S  R  R  N  B  D  L  I  E  O  A  R  I  E
P  U  C  C  I  N  I  S  N  S  A  V  D  A  N
O  M  E  N  D  E  L  S  S  O  H  N  I  H  E
K  A  R  O  V  D  G  I  K  E  B  R  U  C  H
I  C  H  O  P  I  N  D  Y  A  H  N  E  T  H
M  K  V  S  A  I  N  T  S  A  E  N  S  G  E
```

BACH	DVORAK	MENDELSSOHN	SHOSTAKOVICH
BEETHOVEN	FIELD	MOZART	SIBELIUS
BERLIOZ	GRIEG	MUSSORGSKY	STRAUSS
BIZET	HANDEL	PUCCINI	STRAVINSKY
BRAHMS	HASSE	RAVEL	TCHAIKOVSKY
BRUCH	HAYDN	ROSSINI	VERDI
CHOPIN	LISZT	SAINTSAENS	VIVALDI
DEBUSSY	MAHLER	SCHUBERT	

Word Search 3

Feel free to zoo-m through the animals hidden in the grid below.

```
C O E E Z N A P M I H C N N E
P N A F L A M I N G O O P O S
E T O Y O C N A T U G N A R O
A U S S W O C O O A O T T E R
C O U L I U P U R N P G P P E
O O M O O B A D T A O I O I C
C R A T M D O A O R H R R V O
K A T H N D E D I A A A C D N
V G O A O T L L S V T F U R I
U N P M E H L E E N E F P A H
L A O O E A A E M P E E I P R
T K P N O E L E M A H C N O A
U G P K O F R O G U C A E E E
R A I E R I G Z E B R A N L B
E I H Y W I L D E B E E S T O
```

AOUDAD	FLAMINGO	LEOPARD	TAPIR
BEAR	FROG	LION	TORTOISE
BISON	GIRAFFE	MONKEY	TOUCAN
CAMEL	GORILLA	ORANGUTAN	VIPER
CHAMELEON	HEN	OTTER	VULTURE
CHEETAH	HIPPOPOTAMUS	PANDA	WILDEBEEST
CHIMPANZEE	IGUANA	PEACOCK	ZEBRA
COW	KANGAROO	PORCUPINE	
COYOTE	KOMODO DRAGON	RHINOCEROS	
ELEPHANT	LEMUR	SLOTH	

Word Search 4

Hopefully you won't be interrupted in your intention to find these inter- words!

```
S  N  R  N  N  E  N  I  W  T  R  E  T  N  I
T  I  K  N  I  N  I  N  T  E  R  J  E  C  T
T  I  N  T  E  R  S  T  A  T  E  N  I  E  A
D  N  D  E  T  A  L  E  R  R  E  T  N  I  E
E  T  E  A  R  E  A  R  O  I  R  E  T  N  I
S  E  I  E  E  N  C  T  E  E  R  E  T  N
R  R  K  N  I  L  R  E  T  N  I  V  R  E  T
E  J  D  R  N  N  E  D  N  E  R  R  C  R  E
P  O  E  E  T  R  T  E  N  E  M  A  O  F  R
S  I  N  T  E  R  N  E  T  I  F  M  M  E  P
R  N  R  N  R  I  I  N  R  R  E  F  E  R  O
E  E  E  I  R  I  I  E  E  E  T  E  S  E  L
T  D  T  T  E  R  T  T  E  T  S  R  P  D  A
N  T  N  L  D  N  N  S  N  R  E  T  N  I  T
I  V  I  N  I  I  N  T  E  R  L  E  A  V  E
```

INTERCEDE	INTERIOR	INTERNED	INTERSPERSED
INTERCOM	INTERJECT	INTERNET	INTERSTATE
INTEREST	INTERJOINED	INTERNS	INTERTWINE
INTERFACE	INTERLEAVE	INTERPOLATE	INTERVENE
INTERFERE	INTERLINK	INTERRED	
INTERIM	INTERNAL	INTERRELATED	

Word Search 5

Quick! Hopefully this will quench your thirst as you quest to find all these words!

```
Q Q T N I A R T A U Q C N A I
Q U E S T I O N H T O U Q O Q
T I U R Q Q N E E U Q D N E
E N R E U U U A Q T U N E I L
H I O V A A E Q I O Z V P U P
C N R I R D R U T I I Q U Q U
I E N U T R Y I E T U U R U T
U T Q Q Z A E E A U Q A D A N
Q U I C K N T T A Q S C A R I
U R I T T G I O R A C K U T U
A Q I D A L A U U A O U Q I Q
N U Y S A E U Q U Q U E N C H
T L I U Q Q A L I A U Q Q Q Q
U N Q U A N T I T Y K R I U Q
M C Q U A Y F I T N A U Q L L
```

QADI	QUANTUM	QUERY	QUIRK
QAT	QUARTER	QUESTION	QUIVER
QUACK	QUARTIC	QUEUE	QUIZ
QUADRANGLE	QUARTZ	QUICHE	QUOTATION
QUADRUPED	QUASAR	QUICK	QUOTE
QUAIL	QUATRAIN	QUIET	QUOTH
QUAINT	QUAY	QUILT	QUOTIENT
QUALITATIVE	QUEASY	QUININE	
QUANTIFY	QUEEN	QUINOA	
QUANTITY	QUENCH	QUINTUPLE	

Word Search 6

A sharp eye will be instrumental in finding all of the words in this grid!

```
A I S F H A R P P U S L Y R E
N U C I I T L P I A N O O T N
I B N O I D R O C C A A E G O
R A O E R O D K I E C P L N H
A F A J T N B L L V M O N I P
C R C E N U E E E U C E L L O
O E I O T A L T R K A Z O O L
C N N B T E B T E F S E R I Y
L C O O K P A N A L T N A V X
A H M U H I S I B U A O T O U
R H R T N P S P M T N B I R N
I O A L I G O R I E E M U A D
N R H E E A O X R R T O G T R
E N L L O B N I A I S R V I U
T N I L O D N A M S O T T S M
```

ACCORDION	FIDDLE	MANDOLIN	TROMBONE
BAGPIPE	FLUTE	MARIMBA	TRUMPET
BANJO	FRENCH HORN	OBOE	TUBA
BASSOON	GLOCKENSPIEL	OCARINA	UKELELE
CASTANETS	GUITAR	ORGAN	VIOLA
CELLO	HARMONICA	PIANO	VIOLIN
CLARINET	HARP	PICCOLO	XYLOPHONE
CORNET	KAZOO	SACKBUT	
DRUM	LYRE	SAXOPHONE	

Word Search 7

We hope you found the zone as you finished your zealous pursuit of these words!

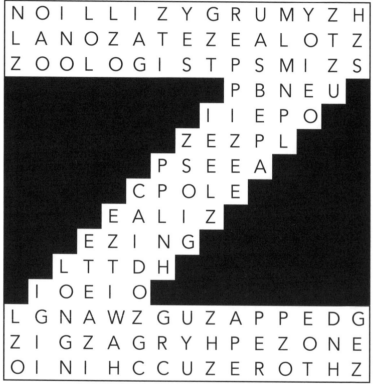

```
N O I L L I Z Y G R U M Y Z H
L A N O Z A T E Z E A L O T Z
Z O O L O G I S T P S M I Z S
              P B N E U
              I I E P O
            Z E Z P L
          P S E E A
        C P O L E
      E A L I Z
    E Z I N G
  L T T D H
I O E I O
L G N A W Z G U Z A P P E D G
Z I G Z A G R Y H P E Z O N E
O I N I H C C U Z E R O T H Z
```

ZAPPED	ZEPPELIN	ZIPS	ZUCCHINI
ZAPS	ZEROTH	ZIT	ZUGZWANG
ZEALOT	ZETA	ZODIAC	ZYGOTE
ZEALOUS	ZIG ZAG	ZOMBIE	ZYMURGY
ZENITH	ZILLION	ZONAL	
ZEOLITE	ZING	ZONE	
ZEPHYR	ZIPPER	ZOOLOGIST	

Answer Keys

Sudoku 1

1	7	4	2	9	3	6	8	5
9	2	6	5	8	4	7	3	1
5	8	3	1	6	7	4	9	2
4	5	1	9	2	8	3	7	6
2	6	9	3	7	1	8	5	4
7	3	8	6	4	5	2	1	9
3	9	7	4	1	6	5	2	8
8	4	2	7	5	9	1	6	3
6	1	5	8	3	2	9	4	7

Sudoku 2

4	9	7	5	1	8	3	6	2
8	5	6	2	4	3	9	1	7
2	1	3	6	7	9	5	4	8
6	2	4	9	8	5	1	7	3
1	7	8	4	3	2	6	5	9
5	3	9	1	6	7	2	8	4
3	6	5	8	9	4	7	2	1
9	8	1	7	2	6	4	3	5
7	4	2	3	5	1	8	9	6

Sudoku 3

8	3	1	5	6	2	4	7	9
7	4	9	8	3	1	6	5	2
5	2	6	9	4	7	1	3	8
6	7	8	2	5	3	9	1	4
3	1	2	4	9	8	5	6	7
9	5	4	7	1	6	8	2	3
4	6	3	1	7	9	2	8	5
2	9	7	6	8	5	3	4	1
1	8	5	3	2	4	7	9	6

Sudoku 4

5	7	3	8	6	1	2	4	9
9	2	8	3	4	5	1	7	6
1	6	4	7	2	9	8	3	5
8	3	6	4	1	2	9	5	7
2	5	7	9	8	6	3	1	4
4	9	1	5	3	7	6	2	8
6	4	9	2	7	3	5	8	1
3	8	5	1	9	4	7	6	2
7	1	2	6	5	8	4	9	3

Sudoku 5

6	4	3	2	5	1	9	7	8
5	2	7	8	4	9	1	3	6
1	9	8	7	3	6	2	5	4
8	7	6	9	1	2	3	4	5
9	5	1	3	8	4	6	2	7
4	3	2	5	6	7	8	1	9
2	6	9	4	7	3	5	8	1
3	8	4	1	9	5	7	6	2
7	1	5	6	2	8	4	9	3

Sudoku 6

5	1	2	3	9	8	7	6	4
4	3	9	7	5	6	2	1	8
6	8	7	4	1	2	9	3	5
7	2	1	9	3	5	8	4	6
8	6	3	2	4	7	5	9	1
9	5	4	8	6	1	3	7	2
1	7	6	5	8	3	4	2	9
2	9	8	1	7	4	6	5	3
3	4	5	6	2	9	1	8	7

Sudoku 7

1	7	3	9	2	8	6	5	4
2	8	4	6	5	7	3	1	9
6	9	5	1	4	3	2	7	8
7	5	8	2	6	1	4	9	3
4	3	6	5	7	9	1	8	2
9	1	2	3	8	4	7	6	5
3	4	7	8	9	6	5	2	1
8	2	1	7	3	5	9	4	6
5	6	9	4	1	2	8	3	7

Sudoku 8

8	6	7	9	1	4	2	5	3
9	2	3	7	5	6	4	8	1
1	5	4	3	8	2	9	7	6
2	9	5	8	4	1	3	6	7
3	1	6	5	9	7	8	2	4
4	7	8	6	2	3	1	9	5
5	3	2	4	6	8	7	1	9
6	4	1	2	7	9	5	3	8
7	8	9	1	3	5	6	4	2

Sudoku 9

4	6	3	9	5	8	7	1	2
7	2	9	4	1	6	3	8	5
1	8	5	7	2	3	4	6	9
8	9	2	3	6	5	1	4	7
3	1	7	8	4	2	9	5	6
5	4	6	1	7	9	8	2	3
6	7	8	5	3	4	2	9	1
9	5	1	2	8	7	6	3	4
2	3	4	6	9	1	5	7	8

Sudoku 10

3	6	5	9	7	1	2	4	8
2	1	9	4	6	8	3	7	5
7	8	4	5	3	2	9	1	6
1	9	8	6	2	7	4	5	3
4	2	6	3	1	5	8	9	7
5	7	3	8	4	9	1	6	2
8	3	7	1	5	4	6	2	9
9	4	2	7	8	6	5	3	1
6	5	1	2	9	3	7	8	4

Sudoku 11

7	4	3	2	6	8	9	5	1
5	8	2	3	1	9	6	7	4
6	1	9	4	5	7	8	2	3
9	7	6	8	3	5	4	1	2
3	2	8	1	7	4	5	6	9
4	5	1	9	2	6	3	8	7
2	6	4	5	9	1	7	3	8
1	9	7	6	8	3	2	4	5
8	3	5	7	4	2	1	9	6

Sudoku 12

6	5	9	1	7	8	2	3	4
3	4	1	9	6	2	5	7	8
7	8	2	3	4	5	6	9	1
8	9	3	4	5	6	7	1	2
1	7	4	2	9	3	8	5	6
2	6	5	8	1	7	9	4	3
4	1	6	7	8	9	3	2	5
5	2	7	6	3	1	4	8	9
9	3	8	5	2	4	1	6	7

Mastermind 1

A A F

Mastermind 2

G B F

Mastermind 3

C D G F

Mastermind 4

C L E A R

Mastermind 5

E A A F

Mastermind 6

J A D E D

Mastermind 7

H B C E D

Mastermind 8

D B C D F

Mastermind 9

E C I C D

Mastermind 10

Y Y Y Y Y

Mastermind 11

C A G E D

Fill-In 1

Fill-In 2

Fill-In 3

Fill-In 4

Fill-In 5

Fill-In 6

Fill-In 7

Fill-In 8

Fill-In 9

Fill-In 10

Catwalk 1

Catwalk 2

Catwalk 3

Catwalk 4

Catwalk 5

Catwalk 6

Catwalk 7

Catwalk 8

Catwalk 9

Catwalk 10

Catwalk 11

Catwalk 12

Catwalk 13

Easy as ABC 1

E	A	C	B	D
B	E	A	D	C
A	C	D	E	B
C	D	B	A	E
D	B	E	C	A

Easy as ABC 2

Easy as ABC 3

Easy as ABC 4

Easy as ABC 5

Easy as ABC 6

Easy as ABC 7

Easy as ABC 8

Easy as ABC 9

Grades 1

Grades 2

Grades 3

Grades 4

Grades 5

Grades 6

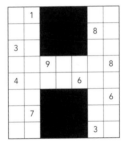

Grades 7

		3					
1					4		
		1		5			
							9
	2				6		
			5				3
5							
		8			9		

Grades 8

			8				
6						7	
			2				
					4		
		5					3
1							
				9			
	3					7	

Grades 9

		2		4			1
	5						
			9		5		
		4					
6				3			
		8					
	7						5
		1		1			

Grades 10

Grades 11

		1		1			
1						1	
	1		1				
1							1
	1		1		1		
1							
		1		1			
	2					1	
		1		1			

Grades 12

		7					6
4				3			
						8	
	9		1				
					4		
5							2
				2			
	7					7	

Grades 13

		4		1			
1					9		3
		7					
1					9		6
	9		5				
6						9	
		3		9			
	8						3
		1		8			

Kakuro 1

Kakuro 2

Kakuro 3

Kakuro 4

Kakuro 5

Kakuro 6

Kakuro 7

Kakuro 8

Kakuro 9

Magnets 1

Magnets 2

Magnets 3

Magnets 4

Magnets 5

Magnets 6

Magnets 7

Magnets 8

Mintonette 1

Mintonette 2

Mintonette 3

Mintonette 4

Mintonette 5

Mintonette 6

Mintonette 7

Mintonette 8

Word Search 1

Word Search 2

Word Search 3

Word Search 4

Word Search 5

Word Search 6

Word Search 7

Exercise Your Mind at American Mensa

At American Mensa, we love puzzles. In fact, we have events—large and small—centered around games and puzzles.

Of course, at 55,000 members and growing, we're much more than that, with members aged 2 to 102 and from all walks of life. Our one shared trait might be one you share too: high intelligence, measured in the top 2 percent of the general public in a standardized test.

Get-togethers with other Mensans—from small pizza nights up to larger events like our annual Mind Games—are always stimulating and fun. Roughly 130 Special Interest Groups (we call them SIGs) offer the best of the real and virtual worlds. Highlighting the Mensa newsstand is our award-winning magazine, *Mensa Bulletin*, which stimulates the curious mind with unique features that add perspective to our fast-paced world.

And then there are the practical benefits of membership, such as exclusive offers through our partners and member discounts on magazine subscriptions, online shopping, and financial services.

Find out how to qualify or take our practice test at americanmensa.org/join.

AARP Resources for Brain Health

Staying Sharp (www.stayingsharp.org)
AARP's Staying Sharp provides evidence-based information and actions you can take to maintain and improve your brain health as you age. Staying Sharp follows guidance from the Global Council on Brain Health to offer:

- **Articles** on how to protect and strengthen your brain
- **Activities** that fit into your daily life
- **Recipes** to nourish your brain
- **Videos** to learn what's good for your brain
- **Brain games** that are challenging and fun
- **Brain health assessment** to understand cognitive skills and how lifestyle supports brain health

Global Council on Brain Health (www.GlobalCouncilonBrainHealth.org)
Convened by AARP, the Global Council on Brain Health is an independent collaborative, created to provide trusted information on how you can maintain and improve your brain health. Its clear and dependable guidance is based on the foremost thinking from scientists, doctors, scholars, and policy experts around the world. Council members debate the latest in brain health science to reach consensus on what works and what doesn't. Its overriding goal is to help people apply the latest scientific insights to boost their cognitive health and live their best lives.

With a nationwide presence and nearly 38 million members, AARP (www.aarp.org) is the nation's largest nonprofit, nonpartisan organization dedicated to empowering people 50 and older to choose how they live as they age.